After the Tassel Is Moved

Guidelines for High School Graduates

Revised Edition

Louis O. Caldwell

BAKER BOOK HOUSE

Grand Rapids, Michigan 49516

First edition, twenty-seven printings

Revised edition
ISBN: 0-8010-2553-2

Fifth printing, January 1995

Printed in the United States of America

All Scripture quotations in this publication, unless otherwise marked, are from the Holy Bible, New International Version. Copyright © 1973, 1978, 1984, International Bible Society.

The recollections of a gifted young lady (pp. 13 and 14) are those of Mary Libbey in the June 1963 *Reader's Digest*. Reprinted from the Fort Collins, Colo., High School *Myriad*. Used with permission of The Reader's Digest Association, Inc.

The poem "Perspective" by Bob Benson (pp. 46–47) is reprinted from the *United Evangelical Action*. © 1963 and used with permission.

The selection from "The Road Not Taken" (p. 55) is from the *Complete Poems of Robert Frost*. © 1916 by Holt, Rinehart and Winston, Inc. © 1944 by Robert Frost. Reprinted by permission of Holt, Rinehart and Winston, Inc.

The quotation of Carl Sandburg (p. 71) is from "Prayers of Steel." © 1918 by Holt, Rinehart and Winston, Inc. © 1946 by Carl Sandburg. Reprinted by permission of Holt, Rinehart and Winston, Inc.

The excerpt by J. Wallace Hamilton (p. 71) is from *The Thunder of Bare Feet*. © 1964 by Fleming H. Revell Company and used with permission.

The budget chart (p. 82) is adapted from *So You're Going to College*, published by the Sun Life Insurance Company of Canada.

TO
the cherished memory
of my grandparents
Mr. & Mrs. O. W. McDonald

and

All My Former Students
who have experienced the thrill
of "moving the tassel"

Acknowledgments

Judi Walker	Louis R. Caldwell
Peggy Brown	David A. Caldwell
Nellie Gabbard	Paul B. Caldwell
Shizuka Kasai	Kristi Gibson
Donald A. Bass	Mona Steward
Mamie Caldwell	Charles Dye
Terri L. Caldwell	Clint Hendricks

Contents

Preface to the Second Edition

Soon after I started teaching in the Houston Public School District in 1958, I began to receive invitations to the graduation exercises of my former students. Little did I realize what those invitations were leading me to!

Of course, each invitation brought with it the need to give a gift! And I've always believed that books are the best gifts because they keep on giving. So, off to the Christian bookstores I went to find a book that gives a Christian interpretation of high school graduation and guidance for the future.

To my surprise, no such books were available. I still remember standing in the Baptist Book Store on South Main in Houston recalling these words: "A need known and the ability to meet that need constitutes a call." At that sacred moment I was "called" to do my part in meeting the need of providing a Christian book for high school graduates. I went straight home to my study and outlined the book which I titled *After the Tassel Is Moved*. Before long, it was completed and sent to Baker Book House. It was published the following spring and immediately became a bestseller.

Recently a lady walked into the waiting room of the Houston Christian Counseling Center, where I am Director. Spotting a copy of *After the Tassel Is Moved*, she asked me, "Are you the author of that book?" I said, "Yes," and then she said, "When I graduated from high school, my parents gave me a copy of your book. And now my daughter is graduating from high school and I'm buying a copy of your book for her!"

And then it hit me. A generation of tassel movers had been receiving my book. It has gone through numerous printings and is nearing one million copies in sales. And it all started the day I received a former student's invitation in the mail.

Although this book has been updated and reprinted many times, its message has not changed. For this new edition, however, another chapter was needed, along with updating and revising the chapters previously written. This additional chapter focuses on the problems of chemical abuse and addiction, and it attempts to explain the Christian way of avoiding and overcoming what has become a nationally destructive problem. If one high school graduate is helped to deal victoriously with any form of addiction as a result of this new chapter, I will be eternally grateful.

This is a good place to express my gratitude also, for the hundreds of thousands of parents, pastors, teachers, relatives, and friends of high school graduates over the years who have given copies of *After the Tassel Is Moved*. Their confidence in my book continues to make me grateful.

1

That Bittersweet Moment

"What kind of book would you appreciate at the time of graduation from high school?"

This was the question I asked high school seniors before preparing this book. To get additional help, I went to some recent tassel-movers and asked them to look back and, in the light of their experiences since graduation, tell me what they would like to have included in a book such as this. Many of the replies were very helpful. Here are a few of the typical ones:

How to be a success
How to choose a college
How to choose a career
How to make decisions regarding marriage
How to enter the future with confidence
How to know God's will for my life

Not only were they as high school seniors quite sure of the kind of information they wanted, but they also had definite ideas as to the way in which it should be presented. "Please don't overstress the solemn facts, responsibilities, obligations, and pressures that face us," they pleaded. "It's not that we don't want to face up to our future, but if the picture is painted too black, we're apt to think that the challenge is too great." Another common request was, "Let us know what's ahead. Be realistic without being preachy."

These questions and concerns, however, have not been the only guidelines for writing this volume. More than anything else I wish to share a deep conviction that the high school graduate should be aware of Christ's presence, promises, power, and claims. All those wearing the cap and gown who recognize their need of divine guidance, and who seek earnestly to know and realize God's will for their lives, can be assured of having the living Christ actively enter into their lives!

Granted, there are several million youth who will graduate this year. But you are not lost in the crowd, not to the One of whom it was written: "For he knew all men" (John 2:24b).

You are not only known to him, you are also valued by him:

> Are not five sparrows sold for two pennies? Yet not one of them is forgotten by God.
> Indeed, the very hairs of your head are all numbered. Don't be afraid; you are worth more than many sparrows.
> —Luke 12:6, 7

Christ knows you as an individual and is aware of what your graduation means to you.

Remember how it was? You heard your name called and suddenly the moment had come. Your parents, teachers, friends, and fellow classmates watched as you strode across the platform to receive your diploma. Amid the camera flashes and applause you shook hands with your principal and accepted the symbol of having satisfactorily completed the equivalent of twelve years of formal education.

As you walked off the platform your next act was deeply meaningful. You took your tassel and moved it over to the left-hand side of your cap. A new milestone in your life had been reached and you knew that feeling, that bittersweet feeling, that mixes the joys and successful struggles of the past with the question marks and challenges of the future.

A gifted young woman looked back from graduation and traced with insight and sensitivity the development of an important realization: "It was one day during the last few weeks of school," she began, "that I first saw her. I was on my way to the library when out of nowhere she came roller-skating down the cracked sidewalk. As I paused to let her go by, memories of my childhood came surging back"—and she recalled a surprising number of memories that made her childhood seem like a magic time.

"The next day I saw her again. She was standing across the street when school let out. After that I saw her every day, sometimes more than once a day. She had long brown-gold curls and wore a pretty little dress which seemed strangely familiar. I never saw her face very clearly—it was always in the shadows. Who was she? Why did I see her so often? I tried to approach her, but when I came near she would run away. She would always come back though and wait somewhere in the shadows. But as graduation drew near, I had little time to wonder about that silent child who waited—for what, I didn't know.

"Commencement night came at last, with its excitement and tension, and a touch of sadness. All day long I had been rushing about, trying to keep out the memories of those past years and the friends I'd be leaving. As I went out of the house something seemed to be missing. I realized I hadn't seen the child all day, and suddenly I felt very lonely.

"The evening passed swiftly. As we turned into the aisle to march out, I looked through the crowd, searching. There she was, sitting by my parents. As she looked at me I saw her face for the first time. In that brief moment I realized who she was and why she was there. An overwhelming sadness passed over me. This was the crossroads; she had come to say goodby."

Concluding her remarks, Mary said, "Perhaps, I would see her again, somewhere in the far distance: but it would never again be as it once had been. Our eighteen years together were ending. I had to go without her. As I went through the door, I took one last look. She was gone. I knew she would be."

Yes, Mary knew and so do you.

A nostalgic look at those wonderful "green years" blends itself with the realization that your achievement represents the combined efforts of a great many people. You were able to move the tassel and to receive the cherished diploma because of the sacrifices and dedication of parents, teachers, counselors— everyone who contributed to your life, many of whom you will never know. Perhaps the most deeply moving of all these realizations is that of having had the unseen help of God whose assistance has been given you in a thousand wonderful ways.

All this and much more was yours at graduation. As memories linger, you can savor with deep understanding the meaning of this scriptural insight: "The longing fulfilled is sweet to the soul" (Prov. 13:19).

2

"Where To Now?"

Looking back at graduation, a young woman recalled " . . . this is the way it was: a time of joy, then the stirrings of doubt . . . goodbye to friends, some forever . . . memory of all the good things, the warm feelings of belonging . . . search for knowledge revealing frightening new lands . . . and now . . . where to now?"

Recall how it built up? Maybe it began with receiving your class ring—how proud of it you were! Your high school yearbook finally came off the press and you began collecting as many signatures of classmates and teachers as possible. Then you were mailing your invitations and ordering your cap and gown. Applications to colleges and universities or for employment were being filled out, and replies were anxiously anticipated. Final exams were ahead, and the tension mounted.

Now that you have made it, you are in the company of thousands of others who stand with diplomas in hand, asking the question, " . . . and now . . . where to now . . . ?"

17

The Bible records the famous words of the wisest man in the world of his day: "There is a time for everything, and a season for every activity under heaven" (Eccles. 3:1). Now, at graduation, is the "time and the season" for deciding which direction your life will take and how you will prepare for what looms ahead.

A story is told about a sailor shipwrecked on one of the South Sea Islands. The natives found him, lifted him to their shoulders, and carried him into their village. Little hope was held by the sailor as he imagined himself being served "well-done" to the natives that night at dinner.

His worries were replaced by astonishment, however, when they placed him on a throne and put a crown on his head. He was then proclaimed their king. The natives became his servants; his every wish was their command. For a while the sailor took full advantage of his new kingly status. But as time passed he began to wonder about it all.

Discreetly he questioned a few of the natives, and what he discovered came as a jolt. It seemed that each year the natives practiced a custom of making some man a king. He "reigned" one year, at the end of which time he was banished to an island and left there to starve to death.

Immediately the sailor began to ponder the future! He was a clever, resourceful fellow and soon came up with a brilliant solution. "Since I am still king," he reasoned, "the natives are still my servants. First, I'll have them build some boats. After they've done that, I'll have them take fruit trees to the island where they plan to send me. There they can transplant the fruit trees, build some nice houses, clear some land, and plant crops."

The commands were given and obeyed. At the end of his year as king, the natives were true to their custom. Only this time the banished "king" did not starve to death, thanks to his wise planning ahead!

What is the wisest way to plan for your future? Consider these two suggestions: (1) know where the rocks are and (2) prepare for life's inevitable experiences.

"My interest is in the future," said Charles F. Kettering, "because I am going to spend the rest of my life there." An interest in the future is important but more is needed: courage and direction are also essential. Facing the uncertainty of the future you find yourself identified with those who belonged to the Hebrew nation of long ago that camped on the brink of the Promised Land. There the Israelites received instruction from their new leader, Joshua, that by following the ark carried by the priests ". . . you will know which way to go, since you have never been this way before" (Josh. 3:4).

How modern and meaningful are the words, "since you have never been this way before." How can you know the way? "After the tassel is moved," how do you know which step to take next?

Perhaps this story can help guide us. Three fishermen were anchored about a football field's distance off shore and were catching only a few fish. One of the anglers decided that he would go ashore. He stepped over the side and walked across the water to the beach. No sooner had his feet touched the sand when another of the men announced that he too would go ashore. As the third man looked on with astonishment, his buddy duplicated the performance of the first man.

"Well," thought the man who remained in the boat, "if they can do it, so can I." And over the side he went and straight to the bottom he plunged. He came splashing back to the surface and climbed back into the boat. But he was not one to give up too quickly. Again he tried but with the same results.

The two men standing on the shore had been observing the futile efforts of their friend and were so weak from laughter they could hardly stand. Finally one managed to say to the other, "He'll drown himself if we don't hurry and tell him where the rocks are!"

Your future's surface covers the "rocks," the principles of a meaningful, effective, creative life. You do not have to have 20/20 vision to observe how often the rocks are missed. Conformity to conduct codes of today are not reliable supports or guides; cultural standards are a tide that changes and washes away faulty foundations.

Ann Landers, whose column is read by thousands of youth, knows where the "rocks" are. She wrote: "The answer to every problem can be found between the covers of the Bible." The great Christian educator, William Lyon Phelps, professor of English at Yale, for many years used to tell his students, "I would rather have a knowledge of the Bible without a college education than a college education without a knowledge of the Bible." My own conviction as a former teacher of secondary-school youth, professor of psychology for almost twenty years, and counselor for more than twenty-five years is that as you stand at your new stage in life, the Bible is your best source of help. The eternal promises and principles found in God's Word will safely guide you into your future. They will chart a course approved by God. The Creator of the terrain is best qualified to give reliable directions. The Divine Mapmaker has done his part in pointing out "where the rocks are."

So certain is Jesus Christ about the results of living life his way that he ends the greatest sermon ever taught with these words:

> "Therefore everyone who hears these words of mine and puts them into practice is like a wise man who built his house on the rock. The rain came down, the streams rose, and the winds blew and beat against that house; yet it did not fall, because it had its foundation on the rock. But everyone who hears these words of mine and does not put them into practice is like a foolish man who built his house on sand. The rain came down, the streams rose, and the winds blew and beat against that house, and it fell with a great crash."
>
> When Jesus had finished saying these things, the crowds were amazed at his teaching, because he taught as one who had authority, and not as their teachers of the law.
>
> —Matthew 7:24-29

To those who question the authority of his words, Jesus says, "My teaching is not my own. It comes from him who sent me. If anyone chooses to do God's will, he will find out whether my teaching comes from God or whether I speak on my own (John 7:16, 17).

Following the directions of the inspired Scriptures you can be secure in the knowledge that when you take the next step into your future you will feel a rock underfoot!

The second principle of successful planning is that of preparing for life's inevitable experiences.

Long ago there lived a man named Saint Philip Neri, whose ability to teach law was known far and wide. Eager young students would travel great distances to receive his instruction. He had an entrance exam that he gave each new student.

"Why did you come?" he would begin.

"To study law," was the standard reply.

"What will you do when you have studied law?"

"I will set up my practice."

"And after that?"

"I will get married and have a family."

"What then?"

"I will enjoy my home and my work."

"Then what?"

"Then I will grow older and eventually die."

"And after death what then?"

Thus the great teacher would lead the student to the most certain of life's experiences: " . . . man is destined to die once, and after that to face judgment" (Heb. 9:27). Saint Philip knew that until the student was ready to die, he could not truly be ready to live. Alexander Dumas put it like this: "If the end be well, all is well."

The happiest, most effective life is lived by those who recognize life's "common ventures" (such as death, work, marriage, and parenthood) and prepare adequately for them. The Chinese have a proverb for it: "Dig your well before you get thirsty." The Bible has an example for it: " . . . the ant . . . has no commanders, no overseer or ruler, yet it stores its provi-

sions in summer and gathers its food at harvest"
(Prov. 6:6–8).

How unlike the ant who looks ahead is the light-
ning bug, about whose frustration an insightful poet
wrote whimsically:

> The lightning bug's plight is a tragic one
> It's been said again and again.
> For he cannot see where he's going;
> He can only see where he's been!

In five or ten or twenty-five years, you will be
"there." The question is, *where?* The answer will be af-
fected by two significant influences: the people with
whom you associate and the books you will read.
From our Christian perspective, your generation has
not received the better advice from many of its
"authorities." For example, some time ago 190 educators and authors were asked what they thought
should be required reading for American high school
students. Their ranking placed Shakespeare's *MacBeth*
and *Hamlet* first; American historical documents, such
as the Declaration of Independence and Lincoln's
Gettysburg Address, second; Mark Twain's *Huckle-
berry Finn* third; and the Bible fourth.

A mother put a twenty-dollar bill in a Bible that she
packed for her son as he left for college. He returned
after the school year was over and, as she helped him
unpack his belongings, she found the Bible with the
twenty-dollar bill still undiscovered! And to think
what else went undiscovered! What about *you* and
your Bible? Are you taking advantage of its unlimited
treasure of wisdom, guidance, and inspiration—all

leading to him who loves you and offers to be your Savior, Lord, and friend?

Looking ahead to the future and wondering which direction to take, you can plan with the greatest confidence if, like the psalmist, you have learned: "Your word is a lamp to my feet and a light for my path" (Ps. 119:105).

3

"A Sheath Without a Sword"

In his poem "The Statue and the Bust," Browning describes a brilliant, talented young aristocrat as "a sheath without a sword." The youth was living a life without purpose. What good is a sheath, regardless of its potential and external attractiveness, and what good is life if it is without a worthwhile purpose?

Jane (not her real name) was a "sheath without a sword." Having graduated from a metropolitan high school with a perfect 4.0 average, she was the valedictorian of her class. She accepted a scholarship from a well-known university, and all who knew her were positive she would succeed.

In the process of enrolling, Jane suffered an emotional breakdown and was advised by a college counselor to return home. After returning home, she attempted to enroll in a large university in her hometown. Again the breakdown occurred. She consulted a doctor, and his examination revealed no organic excuse for her problem.

A third time she attempted to enroll in college. This

time it was a small junior college, and again she lost control.

Needless to say, Jane was in a state of despair. When she came to me to talk about her future, she related how that in junior high school she was denied an award that she felt she had deserved. In her opinion the award was given on the basis of personality. She perceived herself deficient in this area, so she decided to excel academically and drove herself to reach that goal. All her ambition and energy were directed toward reaching that inferior objective. She reasoned that academic honors could not be denied her on the basis of personality. When her goal was reached, however, she discovered that she had nothing definite to look forward to. Lacking a strong enough purpose to continue, Jane found herself emotionally unable to enter college that semester.

Goals make the difference between the drifter and the doer. As someone said, "No wind is favorable if the captain does not know to which port he is steering." Goals give purpose to living. Lacking this purpose, many of today's college-age youth are unable to meet successfully the challenge and struggles of life. For some the frustration and despair become so great that suicide seems to be the only answer. How tragic that any youth should despair of life and come to feel the same as Shakespeare's Hamlet, who cried:

> O God! God!
> How weary, stale, flat and unprofitable
> Seem to be all the uses of this world!
> Fie on it! Ah fie! 'Tis an unweeded garden,
> That grows to seed.
>
> —*Hamlet*, Act I, Scene 2

Recent struggles for political freedom significantly halted suppression in eastern Europe. The heroism displayed by these freedom fighters is comparably matched, according to clear historical evidence, by the dedication of followers of Christ. Consider the valiant group Jesus originally chose. The biblical record or tradition show that James, the brother of Jesus, and James, the son of Zebedee, were murdered by mobs in Jerusalem; Philip, Andrew, Simon the Zealot, and Peter were hanged (Peter, at his own request, was hanged upside down because he thought himself unworthy to be hanged in the same way as his Lord); Matthew was killed with a sword; Bartholomew, flayed alive; Thomas was pierced with a lance; Thaddeus was slain with arrows; Matthias was beheaded. Only one of Jesus' first disciples escaped violent death—John the beloved, who lived out his last years in exile on the island of Patmos.

As the centuries have passed, the record of history continues to show the incomparable commitment that Christ has received from his followers. They have died for him; they have lived for him. To please him was the dominant desire of their lives. Jesus taught his followers to pray, "Your kingdom come, your will be done on earth as it is in heaven" (Matt. 6:10). And wherever on earth this kind of life is being lived, there is an increase in hope, dignity, love, justice, opportunity, and quality of life.

Unlike others who also strive for just causes, the Christian has the advantage of knowing now who belongs to the winning side. "That at the name of Jesus every knee should bow" (Phil. 2:10). And again, "I am the Living One; I was dead, and behold I am alive for evermore" (Rev. 1:18). The open tomb and the thrilling history of the Christian church remind us of him whose way of life lives on and will ultimately triumph!

A story is told of the time when a major oil company was looking for a representative to the Far East. Representatives of the firm approached a missionary and offered him $50,000. The offer was refused. They raised it to $70,000 and again he said no.

When they wanted to know his reason, he replied, "Your price is right, but your job is too small. God has called me to be a missionary."

What has God called *you* to be? You may not be certain of your *place* in life, but you can be certain that you have a *purpose* and that your life is important to God and to humankind. Albert Einstein said, "The man who regards his own life and that of his fellow creatures as meaningless is not merely unfortunate but almost disqualified for life." Carlyle, the essayist, offers this insight: "The man without a purpose is like a ship without a rudder—a waif, a nothing, a no-man." He urges, "Have a purpose in life, and, having it, throw such strength of mind and muscle into your work as God has given you."

Some years ago Dr. Frank Gansaulas, the famous Chicago preacher, was in his study writing a sermon when his nephew, a fine athlete in his early twenties, walked in. He noticed the text of his uncle's sermon: "For this reason . . . I came into the world" (John 18:37).

"Uncle," said the youth, "I wish I knew why I was born." Gansaulas had known that his nephew had been having trouble finding himself. Now, however, he was given the opportunity to speak to the troubled young man when he was in a receptive mood. They talked about life for a while and the nephew left.

He had not walked far when he heard the sound of fire engines. The Old Iroquois Theater was on fire, which eventually took more than five hundred lives. When he arrived at the scene, the nephew noticed a number of people standing helplessly at a balcony window.

Picking up a heavy plank, he raced into the building next to the theater and laid the plank across to the window. Many people were saved by the bridge. During the rescue mission a piece of heavy timber tore loose, knocking the youth to the pavement below. His uncle reached him just before he died and said to him, "Now you know why you were born. You were born to save these people."

Later, Gansaulas was in Europe in a certain hotel. There he met a man in the hotel lobby, and in the course of their conversation Gansaulas mentioned that he was from Chicago. The other man suddenly became hysterical and began muttering something over and over. A man walked up and led his irrational friend away.

After a while the third man and Gansaulas were talking about the sad case. The man explained that his friend had been in Chicago one Saturday and went to the Old Iroquois Theater shortly before the great fire broke out. To escape, the man climbed over many others who were panicking. He managed to get out unharmed but went crazy thinking about the experience. Over and over he was heard to say, "I saved nobody but myself. I saved nobody but myself."

Great frontiers are yet before us. The West Coast youth who was asked about goals was wrong when he replied, "Goals? We've got no goals. Our parents have achieved them all for us." What about the physical frontier of space; the social frontier of freedom and brotherhood; the educational frontier of truth, knowledge, and understanding; and above all, the spiritual frontier of the kingdom of God?

How many times have you said what is commonly known as the Lord's Prayer? Think again of the familiar words: "Your kingdom come, your will be done on earth . . ." (Matt. 6:10).

These are the words Christ taught us to pray. When we repeat them in our prayers we are making a wonderful and majestic plea: that his will and way of life cover the earth, that "man's inhumanity to man" cease, that peace and happiness reign everywhere, that sin and suffering be banished forever.

All who involve themselves in cooperating with God in extending his kingdom find the highest purpose for living that is possible. "The greatest use of life is to spend it for something that outlasts it," said William James. "But how," some may ask, "can I have a sense of individuality—find myself—if I live my life this way?" Christ himself gives the answer to this dilemma:

> For whoever wants to save his life will lose it,
> but whoever loses his life for me and for the gospel,
> will save it.
>
> —Mark 8:35

Everyone needs to be gripped by a deeply absorbing purpose that will give direction, power, and meaning to life. A meaningful life becomes possible when a person believes that activities and relationships are directly and vitally connected to goals. Ambition and responsible behavior result when these goals seem supremely worthwhile and attainable. For the Christian the goal of living life to the glory of God is supremely worthwhile. Is this goal attainable? Get the answer yourself from the final words of the resurrected Christ as recorded in Matthew:

> . . . All authority in heaven and on earth has been given to me. Therefore, go and make disciples of all nations, baptizing them in the name of the Father and of the Son and of the Holy Spirit, and teaching them to obey everything I have commanded you. And surely I will be with you always, to the very end of the age.
>
> —Matthew 28:18–20

4

More Important
Than a Career

A certain high school graduating class chose for its motto:

> Your life is God's gift to you;
> What you do with it is your gift to God.

Many Christian youth who have a deep concern regarding the will of God for their lives frequently ask, "How can I know what kind of work the Lord wants me to do?"

The best counsel at these times is probably this: Be certain that you are giving Christ a fully surrendered life. In obeying him today you will be led into his will for you tomorrow. He can be trusted to guide you in choosing a life's work as surely as he can be trusted as Savior and Lord. Meanwhile, "Whatever you do, work at it with all your heart, as working for the Lord, not for men" (Col. 3:23).

Other suggestions for fulfilling your life's purpose would include: (1) evaluating your interests and hobbies, (2) considering the courses in which you made the best grades, (3) talking to your high school counselor or a Christian educator, and (4) reading books that explain qualifications of employees whose work has special appeal for you.

In the final analysis the important consideration is not the work but the worker. The reason why is dramatically illustrated in the ancient Greek tale of Achilles.

When Achilles was born his mother was told that her son had one of two destinies: he would either live a long, uneventful life of ease or a short life of glory and honor. Not wishing her son to die in his young manhood, Achilles's mother decided to hide him on an island. Nobody but girls lived on the island, so Achilles was dressed like a girl and was thought to be safely hid from harm.

Time passed and then there was war between the Greeks and the men of Troy. Finding themselves in danger of losing, the Greeks sought advice of the oracle as to how they might defeat their enemy. The oracle told them they must have the leadership of Achilles. Of course, no one knew where he was. A shrewd and cunning man named Ulysses was selected to begin the important search.

When at last he came to the island inhabited only by girls, Ulysses disguised himself as a peddler. In his pack he carried beautiful ornaments and trinkets. Mixed with these were some gleaming weapons. True to their character the girls flocked around the gaily colored trinkets. Achilles found the attraction of the swords and shields irresistible. Acting true to his character he began brandishing the swords and fending off imaginary sword thrusts with the shields.

When Ulysses saw that he cried, "Here he is, our hero, Achilles!" Being wise in the ways of men, Ulysses knew that what a person chooses is determined by what he is.

All talk about choosing a life's work does little good without stressing that *character is more important than a career*. You did not have to graduate in the top 10 percent of your class to be able to see how it works. You have heard the word *success* used in frequent conversations and speeches during the last few weeks. Few words can compete with *success* around graduation time, but what is the meaning of the word? Examine the following definitions:

> The superior man makes the difficulty to be overcome his first interest, success comes only later.   —Confucius

> The secret of success is constancy of purpose.
> —Disraeli

> If you wish to succeed in life, make perseverance your bosom friend, experience your wise counselor, caution your elder brother, and hope your guardian genius.   —Joseph Addison

> Success lies not in achieving what you aim at, but in aiming at what you ought to achieve.
> —Anonymous

Notice a point that the definitions have in common: success is not a goal, but the result of developing and exercising qualities of character. In the final analysis success is not what we do, but what we are; not what our actions are, but what our attitudes are. Those who seem to have success did not seek after it, and those who make it their life's aim, seem never to hit the target.

"A man's life," said Jesus, "does not consist in the abundance of his possessions" (Luke 12:15). In the biography section of your school's library you could probably find a biography of David Livingstone, the famous missionary. Few people know that he had a brother, John, who became one of the wealthiest men in Ontario. Both boys grew up together in a Scottish home. Although John and David had the benefits of the same instruction, each set his heart on reaching different goals. John decided to gain wealth; David responded to the command of Christ: " . . . If any one would come after me, he must deny himself and take up his cross and follow me" (Matt. 16:24). John reached his goal and enjoyed a comfortable life of luxury. David reached his goal, too, and after giving his life to convert the heathen in Africa, he died there in a dirty little hut. But which brother had the richer life? When John died, his demise was reported in a few words in the obituary column. Ironically, the only distinction given him was that of identifying him as the brother of David Livingstone!

Rudyard Kipling once addressed a graduation class in Canada. In his speech Kipling cautioned: "Don't put too much emphasis on fame and fortune. Some day you will meet a man who needs none of these things, and then you will know how poor you are."

Winston Churchill was reported to have asked an actress, "Would you marry a man for a million dollars?"

"Of course," she replied.

"For five hundred?"

"Of course not! What do you think I am?"

"We have already established that, my dear," said Churchill. "Now we are only trying to determine the degree."

Someone has pointed out that money will buy

A bed but not sleep
Books but not brains
Food but not appetite
Finery but not beauty
A house but not a home
Medicine but not health
Luxuries but not culture
Amusement but not happiness.

Christian youth must spare themselves the disillusionment that poisons life when love of money motivates the setting of life-goals and the investing of ability, time, and energy. Jesus was not unaware of our materialistic needs. He assured us their satisfaction if our values were properly focused. "Seek first his kingdom and his righteousness, and all these things will be given to you as well" (Matt. 6:33).

If fame and money bring success and happiness, why would a very famous playwright who had both confess, "I suffer great periods of depression." To attempt to lift himself out of his valleys of gloom, he relies mainly on drink and pills. "My intake of liquor," he reveals, "is about a fifth a day—half of a fifth of bourbon and half of a fifth of vodka." Added to that is the problem of insomnia. To get some sleep, says he, "I take up to four sleeping pills." Evidently the man who writes about life has not learned to live it successfully. He admits, "My analyst helps me and without him I'd be sunk. I go to him five times a week."

How to invest his or her life should be the top-ranking concern of every Christian graduate. Basically there are only two ways of investing your life: by getting all you can, or by giving all you can. The greatest authority on the good life advised us as to which way brings the greater rewards. He said, "It is more blessed to give than to receive" (Acts 20:35).

Christian character must express itself through service. Your life's work should be governed by a passion to please Christ, determined by an unreserved surrender to his will, directed by your awareness of need and your ability to meet that need, and energized by the Holy Spirit's daily influence upon your dreams, preparation, associations, and activities. Horace Mann, called by many the father of our American public school system, once said, "Be ashamed to die until you have won some victory for humanity!" Listen to the unknown poet's words:

> There is a voice within you calling,
>   To higher and better things.
> In constant yearning and great
>   Heart burning,
> A beautiful song it sings.
>   'Tis the voice of God
> In your Spirit Life,
>   In your most hidden spring;
> Who can know what you can be
>   And do as a man—
> That's the beautiful song it sings.

5

Consider the Wilderness Way

A drop-out at thirteen! She did it, she said, "to concentrate completely on my goal." Few thirteen-year-olds are that certain about their future. "Even then, I knew exactly what I wanted," she said. Her goal? To sing in opera.

To reach that coveted goal, Roberta Peters had to spend many hours in vocal studies. Three years passed and she was offered the leading role in a Broadway musical. The salary looked astronomical and the lure of Broadway danced before her eyes. But if she signed the contract, it would mean being away from her training for opera for a year or more.

Needing advice, sixteen-year-old Roberta went to her teacher. He counseled her this way: "You are good, Roberta, but you can be better. If you take this detour, you'll never know how far along the straight road you might have gone." She refused the shortcut and four years later made her Metropolitan Opera debut in Mozart's *Don Giovanni*.

"I know what I want, and the sooner I can get it, the better I'll like it; and please don't ask me to wait!"

This is precisely the kind of attitude that develops "detour-takers."

Credit (or discredit) our present-day culture for its influence on strengthening the appeal of the shortcut. Ours has been called the push-button society. The emphasis is on speed and our "computer culture" makes it hard to develop patience. The "itch of the instantaneous" is a disease that is reaching epidemic proportions.

Remember the Red Queen in *Through the Looking-Glass*? Rushing through the Looking-Glass Wonderland with Alice in hand, she kept crying out all the time, "Faster! Faster! Don't try to talk. Faster!" Maybe the Red Queen is another name for our time. We might try to catch our breath long enough to ask if all this activity indicates achievement. You wonder if a certain pilot was speaking of us when in answer to a passenger's question, "How are we doing?" he replied, "We're lost, but we're making good time!"

While some young people in this hurry-hurry-hurry age are tempted to rush into marriage and take shortcuts in education and job preparation, it is uncommon to consider the counsel of Roberta Peters' teacher: "If you take this detour [or shortcut], you'll never know how far along the straight road you might have gone."

"The straight road" has no geometrical significance; rather, it means the best direction to take to reach a worthwhile goal. More often than not, "the straight road" looks like the "long way around."

One of the most remarkable journeys in history is found in the Book of Exodus. Led by the brilliant Moses, the nation of Israel journeyed from Egypt to Canaan, the Promised Land. Allowing twenty miles per day for the average walking time, they should have been able to reach their destination in ten days. How long did it take them? Forty years!

Why? "God led the people around by the desert road toward the Red Sea." (Exod. 13:18). What was the reason for this apparent waste of time? G. Campbell Morgan explains it: "God led them that they might learn the truth about themselves by that long discipline."

Life's most treasured gifts take time to possess. There is no shortcut to Christian character, personality, poise, skill, a trained mind, and cultured maturity. These gifts cannot be hurried. How long, for example, does it take to develop the qualities described in Kipling's unforgettable lines:

If

If you can keep your head when all about you
    Are losing theirs and blaming it on you.
If you can trust yourself when all men doubt you,
    But make allowance for their doubting too;
If you can wait and not be tired by waiting,
    Or being lied about, don't deal in lies,
Or being hated, don't give way to hating,
    And yet don't look too good, nor talk too wise:

If you can dream and not make dreams your
      master;
    If you can think—and not make thoughts your
      aim;
If you can meet with Triumph and Disaster
    And treat those two imposters just the same;
If you can bear to hear the truth you've spoken
    Twisted by knaves to make a trap for fools,

Or watch the things you gave your life to, broken,
    And stoop and build 'em up with worn-out
        tools:

If you can make one heap of all your winnings
    And risk it on one turn of pitch-and-toss,
And lose, and start again at your beginnings
    And never breathe a word about your loss;
If you can force your heart and nerve and sinew
    To serve your turn long after they are gone,
And so hold on when there is nothing in you
    Except the Will which says to them: "Hold on!"

If you can talk with crowds and keep your virtue,
    Or walk with Kings—nor lose the common
        touch,
If neither foes nor loving friends can hurt you,
    If all men count with you, but none too much,
If you can fill the unforgiving minute
    With sixty seconds' worth of distance run,
Yours is the Earth and everything that's in it,
And—which is more—you'll be a Man, my son!

Despite our incredible scientific progress, there is still no coin-operated machine that, if you put a quarter in it, will produce twenty-five-cents worth of wisdom, or any of the other treasured gifts! You have to go "by way of the wilderness" to be able to say:

> I am young enough to have joys and sorrows, deep longings and high dreams, and many, many problems, but old enough to know there is a cause for every joy, a cure for every sorrow, a solution to every problem, and fulfillment for every aspiration.

I am young enough to desire success, but old enough to know it should never destroy health or character.

I am young enough to want money, but old enough to know that true wealth consists not in abundance of things one possesses.

I am young enough to covet fame, but old enough to know that better than fame is the joy of spending oneself in self-forgetful, loving service.

I am young enough to enjoy a good time, but old enough to know one cannot have a good time if pleasure-seeking is put first in life.

I am young enough to be enthusiastic over people and things, but old enough not to let my enthusiasm run away with me.

I am young enough to love to play, but old enough to have learned that most fun is having a hard task and seeing it courageously through.

I am young enough to want to be beautiful, but old enough to know true beauty comes from within.

I am young enough to seek far and wide for the Truth, but old enough to know that it is most often found in being faithful to the task in hand.

I am young enough to make many mistakes, but old enough to learn the lesson, forget the experience, and pass on to better things.

I am young enough to dread pain, sorrow, misfortune, but old enough to be grateful for their chastening, mellowing influence.

I am young enough to long for happiness, but old enough to know it tarries longest with us when we seek it least.

I am young enough to crave true friends, but old enough to appreciate them when I find them.

I am young enough to believe passionately in the goodness of the human heart, but old enough to keep that faith regardless of some disillusionment.

I am young enough to know the meaning of love, but old enough to realize it is life's most priceless possession.

I am young enough to have faith in God, in his goodness, in his loving care over me, in his wise and beautiful plan for my life, but old enough to value this faith as the thing that gives life purpose and makes it worth living.

Said George Henry Lewis: "Many a genius has been slow of growth. Oaks that flourish for a thousand years do not spring up into beauty like a reed."

Those who rush through their period of preparation live to regret it, as the following letter to Abigail Van Buren shows:

Dear Abby: I have a problem that bothers me immensely. We have a new minister whose language is atrocious. I can hardly sit through his sermons anymore. He says, "he done," "had went" and "they is." Abby, don't you think that after four years in Bible college he should be able to do better than that? My ten-year-old son notices these mistakes and mentions them to me. Is there a remedy?

Small Town

Dear Small: I don't know how "small" your town is, but if the people were bigger they could raise enough money to import a more literate minister.

Abby could have added to her answer that the minister might have gone through four years of college, but four years of college had not gone through him! Of course grammatical speech is not a minister's most important asset; he should above all else declare the "full counsel of God." But why can't this be done with grammatical correctness? Talking to his ministerial students over one hundred years ago, C. H. Spurgeon said, "The time is past when ungrammatical speech will suffice for a preacher." Like all other abilities, speaking correctly takes time and effort to develop.

The "way of the wilderness" is another name for being able to postpone satisfaction of some present need to attain a more worthy goal in the future. This requires a high degree of self-discipline, but the rewards make the effort worthwhile.

A full, useful life is the result of a great and wonderful unfolding process. As the Scriptures state, " . . . first the stalk, then the head, then full kernel in the head" (Mark 4:28). Moreover, it is the result of a cooperative endeavor between you and your God. This truth is beautifully expressed in Bob Benson's "Perspective." As you read it, you will be reminded of the reward of "the wilderness way":

God and I raised a flower bed.
He really did the most
I guess.
We used
His soil,
His air,
His water,
His life,
His sun.
My part seemed so trivial that
I said,
"Lord, You take those bulbs and
make them grow right there in the box
out in the garage.
You don't need me, Lord,
You can do it by yourself."
"Oh, no," He said—
"I want to do My part;
I'm waiting to begin,
But you must do yours, too.
You'll have to
dig the bed,
bury the bulbs,
pull the weeds."
So I did my feeble part.
And God took that bulb—
burst it with life,
fed it with soil,
showered it with rain,
grew it with sunshine
until we had a beautiful flower.

And then He seemed to say,
"Your life is like a garden
and if you'd like, we'll make it
a beautiful thing.
"I'll furnish," He said—
"the soil of grace,
the sunshine of love,
the rains of blessing,
the wonder of life.
But you must do the digging."
"Lord," I said, "You just go ahead,
make me what You want me to be;
make me a saint,
give me great faith,
fill me with compassion."
"Oh, no," He said. "You've got to
keep your heart tilled,
hoe the weeds of evil,
chop away the second-best.
I'll make you anything—
Pure,
Clean,
Noble,
Useful,
Anything—
but only if you dig."

6

On Making Decisions

William I. Nichols, a former editor of *This Week Magazine,* said that when he was a boy he used to think that somewhere out ahead lay a magic moment when one would be grown up and know all the answers. Life would be easy when that point was reached. There would be no more doubts, no uncertainties, and in any given situation one would know exactly what to do. Looking back over his experiences, however, he confessed, "The only thing I really learned is that the moment of absolute certainty never comes."

Abbott Lawrence Lowell, former president of Harvard, once said, "The mark of an educated man is the ability to make a reasoned guess on the basis of insufficient information." Good judgment has been defined as "a good batting average in your guesses." Is it this lack of certainty that causes so many to shrink back from decision making?

Since to decide on the basis of insufficient information means to run the risk of being wrong, many look for an easier way in life. Rather than make up their minds and then act, they find it easier to procrastinate, just postpone it a while longer.

The results of this have been expressed in the words of the poet:

> He was going to be all a mortal could be,
>   tomorrow.
> No one should be kinder or braver than he,
>   tomorrow.
> The greatest of workers this man would have been,
>   tomorrow.
> But the fact is, he died and faded from view,
> And all he had left when living was through—
> Was a mountain of things he intended to do,
>   tomorrow.

This kind of thought leads to crippling dependence. The great publisher, Cyrus H. K. Curtis, was talking to his associate Edward Bok, who built the famous Bok Tower. "There are two kinds of people who never amount to much," said Curtis.

"And what are the two kinds?" asked Bok.

Curtis answered, "Those who cannot do what they are told, and those who can do nothing else."

Contrast the above philosophy of playing it safe with that expressed by M. Robins in "The Sin of Inactivity":

> I'd rather be the ship that sails
> And rides the billows wild and free
> Than to be the ship that always fails
> To leave its ports and go to sea.

I'd rather feel the sting of strife
Where gales are born and tempests roar;
Than to settle down to useless life
And rot in dry dock on the shore.

I'd rather fight some mighty wave
With honor in supreme command;
And find at last a well-earned grave,
Than die in ease upon the sand.

I'd rather drive when sea storms blow
And be the ship that always failed
To make the ports where it would go
Than be the ship that never sailed.

Some remind us of the fellow who was a victim of indecisiveness. He went to see a psychiatrist. "So you have trouble making up your mind," said the doctor.

"Well, uh, uh," stammered the fellow, "well, uh, yes and no."

Someone once asked J. L. Kraft, the great manufacturer of cheese, to what he attributed his success. "The ability to make up my mind," replied Kraft. He went on to explain his method: "When I have a decision to make, first, I pray hard. Then I think hard, and when time is about up and I must have the answer, I say 'Lord, now you show me the next thing to do.' Then the first idea that comes into my mind after I have gone through that process is what I take to be the answer. I have been correct a large enough percentage of the time to persuade me that this course is sound."

Notice the steps in Kraft's method: (1) earnest prayer, "I pray hard"; (2) deep thought, "I think hard"; (3) faith and action, "When time is about up and I must have the answer, I say, 'Lord, now you show me the next thing to do.' Then the first idea that comes into my mind . . . I take to be the answer."

Let's take those steps one at a time and examine them more closely. First, the matter of prayer. A great deal of soul-searching takes place in the senior year and after graduation. Important questions such as "Should I go to college?" "If so, where?" "Am I capable of succeeding in college?" "Should marriage come before choice of career or college?" "How will the economy affect my life?"—all these and more fill your mind.

So important are the answers to these questions! The wrong decision will seriously affect your future. How comforting in the face of these uncertainties are the words of Christ to every follower of his:

> Ask and it will be given to you;
> Seek, and you will find;
> Knock, and the door will be opened to you.
> —Matthew 7:7

His will for your life can be known, at least enough of it to guide you in deciding what to do next. It is unthinkable that the Christ of Calvary could want to show us his will less than we desire to know it!

The second step is "Think hard."

Take from all your experiences whatever you think will help. Counsel with those who you think are the best qualified to help you. Consider the alternatives and the consequences of each choice.

Above all, be determined to do what you think will enable you to travel in the direction that leads to becoming more effective in the kind of service for which Christ has given you special gifts. "Consider the paths for your feet and take only ways that are firm" (Prov. 4:26).

Faith and action are the third step. Now comes the "moment of truth." If we wait until all the answers are in, we will never be able to act. However, it is right here at the point of the mind's inability to be certain that faith makes the difference!

If this holds true, then it should follow that a strong relationship exists between faith and achievement. Evidence of this is available. A remarkable study some years ago by S. S. Visher showed that persons listed in *Who's Who in America* came from minister's families about twice as often as from families of professional men in general. A second study by Harvard and Yale, using a different criteria of eminence, showed that missionaries and sons of missionaries led the list.

Using his faith and taking positive action helped one young man as he looked for a job. But he had a problem—one that all young people have in common—inexperience. After thinking about his situation, he placed this ad in a New York paper:

> Inexperience is the most valuable thing a man can bring to a new job. A man of inexperience, you see, is forced to rely upon imagination instead of timeworn routine and formula thinking. If you're in the kind of business that is paralyzed by routine and formula thinking, then I'd like to work with you. . . . Need a man to fill a challenging job?

A chain of photo studios promptly hired him!

Among Christian youth there is much talk about consecrating one's life to this work or that work. Decisions based on work will not be as wise as those based on faith—faith in Christ.

"The wise heart will know the proper time ... ," wrote the inspired author of Ecclesiastes (8:5). The importance of this time in your life calls to mind these provocative lines by Shakespeare:

> There is a Tide in the affairs of men,
> Which, taken at the flood, leads on to fortune;
> Omitted, all the voyage of their life
> Is bound in shallows and in miseries.
>   —Julius Caesar, Act IV, Scene 3

Now the "high-tide" time for making important decisions has come, and you are aware of the significance of this time. Friedrich Froebel, German educator and founder of kindergartens, pointed out the importance of such a time:

> Spiritual forces when manifested in man exhibit a sequence, a succession of steps. It follows, therefore, that when a man at one period of his life has omitted to put forth his strength in a work which he knows to be in harmony with the divine order of things, there comes a time, sooner or later, when a void will be perceived; when the fruits of his omitted action ought to have appeared, and do not: they are the missing link in the chain of consequences. The measure of that void is the measure of his past inaction, and that man will never quite reach the same level of attainment that he might have touched, had he divinely energized his lost moments.

Graduation finds you at the crossroads; you must choose which path to take—but which one?

> Two roads diverged in the woods, and I—
> I took the one less travelled by.
> And that has made all the difference.
>   —Robert Frost in *The Road Not Taken*

The road that makes "all the difference" stretches out before you. John Oxenham, an English businessman and writer, called it the "high way" when he penned these familiar lines:

> To every man there openeth
> A way, and ways, and a way
> And the High Soul climbs the High Way,
> And the Low Soul gropes the Low.
> And in between on the misty flats
> The rest drift to and fro,
> But to every man there openeth
> A High Way and a Low.
> And every man decideth
> The way his soul shall go.

An impressive young man who wanted to take the "high way" to success walked up to Norman Vincent Peale—the famous author-minister—and said, "I've got a statement to make and a question to ask."

"Let's have them both," said Dr. Peale.

"First, I want a great future, and, second, I want to know how to make a good start," stated the young man.

Dr. Peale then asked, "And what kind of a future is that?" Some discussion followed as they worked toward a clearer understanding of what the young man really wanted to do with his life.

"Now," said Dr. Peale, "*when* do you want this great future to start?"

"Well," he replied, "sometime soon."

"That great future you want needs to start *now*," Dr. Peale challenged. He then shared with his young inquirer his famous ten-word formula for having a great future: "I can do all things through Christ who strengthens me" (Phil. 4:13, NKJV).

He urged the young man to place copies of this great verse all around him—on his bathroom mirror, in his car, on his desk, and wherever else he could do this. Dr. Peale assured him that with this powerful truth growing in his mind, he could be confident of having that great future.

And you, too, can be confident of having that great future by taking the "high way." You will need divine direction as you travel, and you can have it as you listen carefully: ". . . your ears will hear a voice behind you, saying, 'This is the way, walk in it'" (Isa. 30:21).

7

How Far to Turn the Screw

Over one-hundred years ago, a young man from western Pennsylvania heard of Princeton University's president and was so deeply impressed that he decided to enroll in the university. He took the entrance examination and failed. However, he paid President McCosh a visit before returning home.

When the president answered the door, the young man told him of his desire to enter Princeton, but that, having failed the entrance exam, he was now returning home. "But I would like to thank you," said the youth, "for what I have learned here."

President James McCosh, somewhat startled, said, "Mon, what have ye learned from us?"

"How little I know," answered the youth.

"Mon, we will take ye," replied President McCosh. "Ye are two years ahead of the rest of them."

How many in your graduating class could appreciate what the famous Scottish president of Princeton had recognized in that young man? Having some knowledge of the vast difference between what you know and how much there is yet to learn will indeed mark you as a knowledgeable person.

> We have not yet arrived
> Without this growing notion:
> Our knowledge is a drop;
> Our ignorance an ocean.

Few would debate the importance of humility regarding how much we know. But we dare not stop here; we must go on to think deeply about another point contained in a story that comes from the business world.

A computer broke down and all the geniuses on the office staff tried to fix it. After their unsuccessful efforts, an expert was called in. He turned the machine on and listened to it for a few minutes. Then he took out a screw driver and turned one screw a half turn and, just like that, the machine was repaired.

When the company received a bill for $175.00 at the end of the month, the office manager went into a rage. He demanded an itemized statement to explain exactly what the expert had done.

A few days later, the company received an itemized statement that read: "For turning one screw: 15¢; for knowing how far to turn the screw: $174.85." There is no substitute for practical know-how! The person who knows "how far to turn the screw" will always find opportunities to use his knowledge and skill.

This truth needs to be spread throughout the ranks of today's tassel movers. It is not difficult to find graduates who talk about wanting to help humankind. The problem lies in finding idealistic youth who are willing to subject themselves to the hours and effort required for the development of excellence. Christian youth in particular should understand that just an urge to do some good is not enough.

Can you imagine what would be done to someone who, upon entering the ward for patients about to undergo surgery, would declare while brandishing a scalpel, "I have no medical training, but I do have a burden to help suffering humanity"! When wise King Solomon began work on the magnificent temple, the call went out for workers who were highly trained and skillful: "Send me, therefore, a man skilled to work in gold and silver, bronze and iron, and in purple, crimson, and blue yarn, and experienced in the art of engraving, to work ... with my skilled craftsmen ... " (2 Chron. 2:7).

Talent must be trained; desire must be disciplined. Life can get rough for those who don't know how far to turn the screw. As the Living Bible puts it, "A dull axe requires great strength; be wise and sharpen the blade" (Eccles. 10:10).

You don't need to be reminded that great care should be taken in choosing your work. Nobody wants to be a vocational misfit, and yet many people receive little or no satisfaction from their jobs. For example, a nationwide study made by the American Institute of Public Opinion reveals that about three out of every five workers feel that they are wasting their time in jobs they dislike.

How can this mistake be avoided? Some guidance regarding the problem was offered by John Ruskin, who said: "In order that people may be happy in their work, these three things are needed: they must be fit

for it; they must not do too much of it; and they must
have a sense of success in it."

Let's focus on the first thing Ruskin mentions—
"they must be fit for it." This kind of analysis is not
easy. Matching a person with the work for which he
or she is best suited requires an understanding of the
person as well as the work. Often young people discover interests and abilities by taking vocational tests.
These tests can rate your dexterity, your ability with
numbers and words, and your sense of logic, insight,
and judgment. Your state employment service can
direct you to the proper places to take these tests.
Also, you can take such tests at most colleges and
universities.

For those who will be entering the work force
immediately after graduation, a knowledge of job
trends is valuable. You have graduated from high
school at a time when the need for technical workers
is becoming critical. Openings in this area include
data-processing specialists, electronics technicians,
technical secretaries, lab assistants, supervisors of pro-
duction control, technical photographers, and govern-
ment safety inspectors.

Usually there is a shortage of skilled workers:
carpenters, bricklayers, plumbers, electricians,
mechanics, lathe operators, and machinists.

A strong demand will exist for sales and office
workers: typists, secretaries, clerical workers, and
retail and wholesale sales representatives.

Other openings will be available for service
workers: cooks, waiters and waitresses, police
officers, fire fighters, and hair stylists.

When the time comes to seek employment it helps
to be aware of some commonsense things about the

interview. Personnel directors responsible for interviewing young people who are looking for jobs seem to agree on basic points. Their advice stresses the following and is worth careful consideration:

1. Develop the fundamental skills of reading, writing, and arithmetic.

2. Dress appropriately when you go job hunting. The "take me for what I am, not for how I look" attitude won't persuade prospective employers to change their policy to suit the applicant. Fashion experts say we dress the way we think and we act the way we dress. Behavioral scientists have found that character correlates with cleanliness and appropriate styles of dress.

3. Show common courtesy. One personnel director of a large company who interviews dozens of young people every day complained of youthful applicants who chewed gum and smoked during interviews!

4. Go to the interview by yourself.

5. Display the "I really want to work" attitude.

6. Understand the principle of first things first. You don't need to ask about a pension plan in the first interview.

7. Answer all questions on the application. If you can't respond to a question, put a dash beside it so the personnel director will know you didn't overlook it.

8. Be on time. Punctuality reflects consideration for the personnel director and shows that you are a person with a sense of responsibility.

9. Write or print legibly. Carelessness in this matter wastes the personnel director's time.

10. Remember to trust Christ to help you. He knows the anxieties of young job hunters. Having a sense of his presence will steady you.

According to an ancient Persian proverb:

He who knows not, and knows not
    That he knows not,
        Is a fool,
            Shun him;
He who knows not, and knows that he knows not,
        Is a child,
            Teach him;
He who knows and knows not that he knows,
        Is asleep,
            Wake him;
He who knows, and knows that he knows,
        Is wise,
            Follow him.

Now link the last sentence with this statement by Jesus Christ: "I am . . . the truth . . ." (John 14:6). Startling, isn't it? For not only does it mean that Christ knew and knew that he knew, it also means that he boldly claimed that all knowledge based on truth has its source in *him*. This discovery came to a nineteen-year-old coed who said to me: "Every subject I take— psychology, English, history, or Bible—leads to Christ and reveals more of him."

A clear relationship exists between knowing "how far to turn the screw" and knowing the Source of all knowledge. Read about the education of a youth named Daniel and his friends in the first chapter of the Book of Daniel. There you will find that because they lived godly lives, "To these four young men God gave knowledge and understanding of all kinds of literature and learning . . ." (1:17).

If you have caught the idea that your work is the vocational expression of *you in cooperation with divine purpose*, you are one of the privileged of your generation. This idea elevates and dignifies whatever work you do, and motivates you toward excellence. Further, this idea was held by Christ, as Leslie Weatherhead so beautifully writes:

> See the young man Christ! On the hilltop at night looking into the face of God, the realization of his divine purpose flooding his mind and enflaming his emotions. Then follow him early next morning to his carpenter shop. Watch as he sharpens his tools and lays out plans, throttling down his possibilities to that cottage home and carpenter shop. He is not irked, not resentful. And for 20 years, he faithfully stays with the task.

A concern for the practical is essentially a *Christian* concern, as the poet demonstrates:

> . . . he walked the self-same road,
> And he bore the self-same load,
> When the carpenter of Nazareth
> Made common things for God.

8

What About the Road Ahead?

The last gift to be opened at a bridal shower had a card with it that read, "May this always be so," and was signed, "Much love, Mother and Dad." Inside was a beautifully framed, yellowed piece of paper with childish handwriting on it, which had once been tacked on the bulletin board in the bedroom of the young bride-to-be. There were tears in her eyes as she read to her friends this message:

> Today we had a test in history.
> I have to go to the dentist, too.
> We did not win the paper drive.
> This was the worst day I ever had in my life.

You can appreciate the parents' message: "May this always be so" as being an expression of love. You can also be sure that those same parents knew that the road ahead would not always be smooth.

What about the road ahead? Remember the advice the high school seniors shared with me as I began preparation for this book? "Please don't overstress the solemn facts, responsibilities, obligations, and pressures that face us," they urged. "It's not that we don't want to face up to our future, but if the picture is painted too black, we're apt to think that the challenge is too great."

Some Positive Signs

A good start would be to recognize some positive signs. First is the trend toward simplicity. An encouraging number of respected thinkers believe that in the decade ahead we will see renewed emphasis placed on sincerity, substance, and straightforwardness. It will be a move toward a more casual lifestyle and away from showy pretentions. This "downscaled" way of life will affect what we eat, wear, drive, and read. This encouraging trend will point us away from what will leave people feeling bored, tired, and cheap. A young adult explains the prevailing attitude this way: "I grew up in the '70s and it was a really dispiriting decade for many people. There was one national sadness after another; and I think a lot of people lost a sense of what it meant to have a good time, to enjoy things, and to appreciate things without a great deal of cynicism."

Another good sign is the trend toward traditional values. A growing need is being sensed for a renewed appreciation for the Judeo-Christian values, placing a stronger emphasis on commitment to God, to our fellow human beings, and to the highest and best in each of us. Several years ago a study was made of this nation's National Merit Scholarship winners (and merit scholars come in all sizes, colors, genders, and national backgrounds). The researchers carefully explored all the possible reasons for the outstanding success of these students. They isolated only one factor the winners had in common: Their families sat down to dinner together every night.

Perhaps as a nation we are learning to place greater importance on relationships than on things, to value what lasts more than that which is short-lived, to grasp what enriches quality of life rather than pleasures that degrade, and to appreciate solid preparation for the future more than self-indulgence with its little or no regard for what's ahead. This trend will positively affect marriage, family, work, educational programs, medicine, science, politics, and religion—every phase of our national life.

Some Negative Signs

Serious youth problems are increasing. Look at how problems in public schools have changed over the last forty-five years. In 1940 the top offenses were talking in class, gum chewing, making noise, running in halls, improper dress, and not putting paper in waste baskets. Modern problems include rape, robbery, assault, arson, suicide, drug and alcohol abuse, and pregnancies.

A survey of 39,000,000 American teens revealed that:

65 percent of Christian students are sexually active.

75 percent of high school students cheat regularly.

30 percent of high school seniors have stolen something in the past thirty days.

45 to 50 percent of pregnant teens abort their babies.

3.3 million teenagers are alcoholics.

1,000 teenagers attempt suicide every day.

10 percent of teens have experience with or are living a homosexual life.

The National Institute on Drug Abuse and the National Council on Alcoholism estimate that the average age of first drug use is 13; first use of alcohol is 12. A *Weekly Reader* survey of fourth-graders found that nearly one third were already being pressured by peers to try alcohol and marijuana!

Drug involvement reveals itself by:

An abrupt change in mood or attitude.

Resistance to discipline at home, school, or work—with a sudden decline in performance and attendance.

Heightened secrecy about activities.

Change in choice of friends.

Physical symptoms including dilated or constricted pupils, red eyes, slurred speech, and hyperactivity.

Spiritual symptoms ranging from resistance to church attendance, Bible reading, and prayer to a stubborn rejection of anything religious.

The war on drugs intensifies, currently giving primary attention to cocaine. This highly addictive drug is extremely dangerous, and now with the less expensive "crack" form of cocaine available, the danger is greater than ever.

Users of crack describe what happens when they take this life-threatening drug: their mood is lifted, energy improves, alertness and self-confidence increase. At first there is an intense period of pleasure, which only lasts a few seconds. Then follow several minutes of a less-intense emotional high. Eventually if the user does not take the drug again, "abstinence symptoms" appear, such as depression and loss of energy. So to make these painful emotions go away, the user takes more of the drug. This leads to the deadly cocaine addiction cycle. It becomes an uncontrollable craving and enslaves its abusers.

When senior high school students are asked about their top concerns, two worries tie for first place: being able to pay for college and the fear of contracting AIDS. Next is the fear of making wrong decisions about the future and not being able to change them. The students are fairly pessimistic about the world around them. For example:

- 58 percent do not think there will be an end to racial discrimination in the U. S. in their lifetime.
- 42 percent think there will be nuclear war in their lifetime.
- 62 percent think their lives will be harder than those of their parents.

Our world is changing rapidly. Its resources are shrinking while its population is swelling, especially in economically underdeveloped areas. No longer can we take for granted that we will always have clean air to breathe, pure water to drink, and ample land to use and enjoy. The answer is for each of us to become a better steward of our environment. And we need to start now, where we are, with what we have.

Is the picture all gloom and no gleam? A young woman who was valedictorian of her senior class realized that all individuals must answer for themselves. She began her valedictory address to more than four hundred fellow graduates like this: "Tonight as we stand ready to take our first step down life's pathway, I will ask one question: What will our lives be—a *farce* or a *force*?"

An interesting question! She took the definitions of the words farce and force from Webster:

> Farce: A ridiculous or empty show, something to be laughed at, perhaps ridiculed.
>
> Force: Something that possesses great strength and has a great effect on that with which it comes in contact.

The rest of the address developed the idea that whether one becomes a force or a farce depends upon the way he or she relates to the world. The farces may have impressive intentions, but when faced with difficulty and temptation they give up the fight.

But not so with those who choose to be a force. They are the persons who are unafraid to risk making mistakes, even to fail. These turbulent times may chill the farce but they will challenge the force! Opportunity opens its doors to your generation.

Here and there are heard youthful voices that promise an acceptance of the challenge. One girl hopes that she'll "be elected senator from Oregon. I want to stick pins under people."

Carl Sandburg's request may be shared by more of your generation than some think. He wrote:

Lay me on an anvil, O God.
Beat me and hammer me into a crowbar.
Let me pry loose old walls,
Let me lift and loosen old foundations!

This sounds like New Testament language. J. Wallace Hamilton reminds us:

We who hold this Bible in our hands, we who are followers of the way of Christ are part of the oldest and most radical revolution in human history. It is so old that some of us have forgotten how radical it is, so misshapen that some people are actually shocked to be told that Jesus was a rebel, a revolutionist. So long have they accepted the false picture of a gentle Jesus, meek and mild, that they have forgotten the central fact of our faith: He was executed as an insurrectionist, regarded as an agitator too dangerous to live, and was put to death as a public menace: in His heart was a deep protest against the evils that blight man, and in His mind was a great, thought-out plan for man's salvation.

Compare the Christ with any great person in history and you will recognize him to be the greatest "foundation loosener and lifter" of them all. And as you plan for the future in this uncertain and rapidly changing age, Christ is able to offer you unequaled opportunity to make a meaningful contribution to your world.

9

Questions and Answers

Following are some of the questions most commonly asked by high school graduates. Of course space has limited the scope and content, but perhaps you will find some of the answers helpful.

Q. What kind of specific advice regarding how to become a success can be given?

A. Let William James give this counsel: "Let no youth have any anxiety about the upshot of his education, whatever the line of it may be. If he keep faithfully busy each hour of the working day, he may safely leave the final result to itself. He can with perfect certainty count on waking up some fine morning to find himself one of the competent ones of his generation, in whatever pursuit he may have singled out. Silently, between all the details of his business, the *power of judging* in all that class of matter will have built itself up within him as a possession that will never pass away. Young people should know this truth in advance. The ignorance of it has probably engendered more discouragement and faintheartedness in youths embarking on arduous careers than all other causes put together."

Now the Scriptures: "Constantly remind the people about these laws, and you yourself must think about them every day and every night so that you will be sure to obey all of them. For only then will you succeed" (Josh. 1:8, *The Living Bible*).

Q. I'm trying to decide whether or not to go to college. What information do I need to help me make this decision?

A. When freshmen are asked why they decided to go to college they typically give the following answers:

> To get a better job.
> To acquire a general education.
> To earn more money.
> To please parents.
> To get away from parents.
> To meet interesting people.
> To have something to do.

A significant number of young people entering college will drop out before graduation. Many studies have been made to determine why the drop-out rate is so high. Among the findings that the researchers consistently discover is a lack of purpose in life as it relates to education. Most youth who drop out of college possess enough mental ability to succeed as college students. If they cannot, however, relate their subjects and classroom work to present needs and future goals, then the academic road becomes too rough and leads to no desired destination.

Those who do travel the academic road to graduation often speak of experiencing greater personal growth, a sharper sense of purpose, and a higher development of skills. Any college worthy of the name should offer students the opportunities to discover and develop their abilities so that they can apply themselves at increasingly higher levels of performance to the glory of God.

Two false views of college need to be examined. One view sees going to college as the big cop-out. Those who hold this attitude give reasons that might be classified three ways: (1) Lack of personal freedom: "I don't want to relinquish my personal rights." They chide their friends for going to college just to get parental approval or because most of their friends are going. (2) Lack of purpose: "I'm going because there is nothing better to do." (3) Lack of sense of involvement: "I'm going to escape for a while."

The idea of college being a cop-out seems to be rooted in a belief that instead of contributing to growth, college stifles it. This idea should not be totally rejected, for not all colleges do provide the kind of stimulation and environment that is conducive to personal development. Neither, however, should this idea go unchallenged. Those who hold it seem to be unable to offer convincing evidence that their lifestyle offers much that deserves to be widely imitated.

The second false view—held by many who enroll in college—is that college is the royal route to success. They think, "College will convert me into all I should be." They view college as a cure-all, a guarantee of a secure future.

These false expectations of college are the major reasons for dropping out. Every incoming freshman should know that college should provide the proper environment and opportunities, but the outcome depends on the responses the student makes.

Q. How can I get information on Bible colleges?

A. Some Christian graduates are attracted to Bible colleges. Among the advantages they find are a rich spiritual environment, high academic standards, highly qualified professors, and opportunities for meaningful service. For more information write:

> American Association of Bible Colleges
> 130-F North College St.
> P.O. Box 1523
> Fayetteville, AR 72701

Q. How can I finance a college education?

A. Because of the soaring cost of attending college, few students are able to earn enough money to finance their education. In one three-year period the cost of tuition, room, board, books, and student fees climbed by more than 30 percent. Annual college costs now range from $7,000 to $14,000 for a four-year private school. However, a variety of loan programs are available.

The National Direct Student Loan, presently the loan program with the lowest rate of interest, allows students to borrow up to $6,000. The Guaranteed Student Loan program provides the bulk of loan financing, lending undergraduates $2,500 a year. To qualify for either of these loan programs, families earning more than $30,000 per year must show need by filing a federal form on which the number of dependents, assets, and debts must be declared. The new PLUS program allows parents, regardless of income, to borrow up to $3,000, but at a higher interest rate.

Additional sources of financial assistance can be found among the numerous state-level, college-age assistance programs.

Scholarships may be available to you. Check with your school or community library to acquaint yourself with the commercially published scholarship guides. If you are physically handicapped or a child of a serviceman who was killed or permanently disabled in military action, benefit grants and other special financial aid are available.

The college of your choice probably has an employment service. If the college is located in a large city, employment may not be too difficult to find, but be sure to remember that school comes first!

In his book *Prayer Changes Things,* Charles L. Allen tells about a remarkable minister friend. As a six-year-old boy, Allen's friend was accidentally shot by an older brother. The bullet shot away several fingers of his right hand and permanently impaired the elbow of the other arm.

Time passed and finally the boy graduated from high school. He wanted to go to college but realized that his parents were financially unable to help him. He bought a second-hand typewriter and learned to type. Working as a part-time secretary, he paid for his college education.

Then he went to Yale to obtain a Ph.D. degree. To finance his education there, he worked in the cafeteria and at night read proof in a newspaper office from 11 o'clock until 4 o'clock in the morning. His doctoral dissertation was a study of ninth-century manuscripts written in vulgate Latin, a language he had to learn. He not only had to master vulgate Latin, but before his research could be completed, he had to learn six other languages: Greek, Hebrew, German, French, Aramaic, and Syrian. Not only did he get his Ph.D., he also made an important contribution to biblical knowledge.

When Charles Allen asked his friend how he managed to overcome his handicaps, he replied, "We all have limitations of some kind and we all have abilities. I thought about what I could do and never worried about anything else. Our limitations can be either stepping stones or stumbling blocks."

Q. With college costs rising, I will need to work while I go to school. Are there programs that help you earn money, choose a career, and satisfy employers looking for talent, drive, and experience?

A. Yes, Co-op! Co-op (short for Cooperative Education) is a program linking the classroom with the workplace to provide an education with career relevance. Co-op gives students the opportunity to earn a regular paycheck and get experience in a chosen career at the same time. The best guide to Co-op programs is the *Co-op Education Undergraduate Program Director*, which can be ordered from:

National Commission for Cooperative Education
350 Huntington Avenue
Boston, MA 02115-5005

Q. What is considered for admittance to college?

A. 1. High school grade record.

2. Recommendation of the school principal or counselor.

3. College Board Scholastic Aptitude Test (SAT).

4. Applicant's class standing.

Personal qualities of prospective students are also important to colleges. Admissions offices are concerned about students' character, emotional stability, attitudes, and leadership qualities. Results of personal interviews are included in admission decisions at many colleges.

This indicates that a student's personal character is an important criterion; good scholarship is to be desired, but it is the student's *total* record that colleges evaluate.

Q. Will a college education really increase your earning power?

A. An economist for a life insurance company estimated that for every dollar invested in a college education, the student gets at least twenty to thirty dollars in return.

L. H. Adolfson, of the University of Wisconsin, tells a story that contains excellent guidance for those who wonder if they should have more education. The story is about three horsemen of ancient times who were riding across a desert. As they crossed the dry bed of a river, out of the darkness a voice called, "Halt."

They obeyed. They were told to dismount, pick up a handful of pebbles, put the pebbles in their pockets, and remount.

After they had done as they were instructed, the voice said, "You have done as I commanded. Tomorrow at sun-up you will be both glad and sorry.

The three horsemen rode away thinking about the strange prediction.

The next morning at sunrise, they reached into their pockets and found that a miracle had happened. Instead of pebbles, they pulled out diamonds, rubies, and other precious stones. Then they saw the truth of the prophecy. They were both glad and sorry—glad they had taken some, and sorry they had not taken more.

And this, points out Dr. Adolfson, is the story of education.

Q. I am planning to enter college, and I hope some day to get married and start a family. How would continuing my education affect my chances for future marital success?

A. Very favorably, according to most studies on the subject. Chances for marital success increase with the amount of education acquired by both husband and wife. Higher education will increase your ability to become a good parent, too.

Keep in mind that a few years in college add greatly to your maturity. This means your choice of a marriage mate will be made on the basis of a more mature judgment because of your having developed an "educated" perspective.

Q. Can an average ("C") student succeed in college?

A. High school graduates with a "C" average should not conclude that they are not "smart" enough to succeed in college. Of course, some colleges and universities are highly selective and competition is exceptionally difficult.

Average students are accepted by many good colleges and universities. Don't overlook the community college, for it can serve as an ideal training ground for testing your ability to succeed in college. Often in such a college you will receive greater personal attention from instructors. Many of these schools offer vocational programs that will help you develop "marketable" skills suitable to your style of life and community opportunities.

Average students who possess strong ambition, determination, and a willingness to work hard can succeed in college. Sometimes "C" students in high school become superior students in college!

Q. I'm having trouble getting accepted by a college. What should I do?

A. Apply through one of these nonprofit admission centers:

> American College Admissions Advisory Center
> 2401 Pennsylvania Ave., Suite 1051
> Philadelphia, PA 19130

> Council of Independent Colleges
> One Dupont Circle N. W., Suite 320
> Washington, D.C. 20036

For $1.00 you can receive some excellent information on how to find the right college or university, improve your chances for getting accepted, and how to pay your way. Request the "College Guide" from:

> Reprint Editor
> Reader's Digest
> Pleasantville, NY 10570

Q. After I decide on college, then what?

A. 1. Obtain a catalog of the college or university you want to attend. You will be able to get it from the admissions officer at the college or in a library. Also obtain the catalog of the college of your second choice.

2. Use the catalogs to find out if you will be able to meet the academic standards required for admission.

3. Select two or three specific courses you think you might like to take and for which you will be able to meet the requirements. Do not make a final decision too hastily.

4. Note all dates with respect to enrollment, entrance, and scholarship examinations so that you will be able to complete all forms on time.

5. Make a budget for your first college year as follows:

a.	For tuition (see college catalog)	$
b.	For residence, if any (see catalog)	$
c.	Miscellaneous college expenses (see catalog)	$
d.	Books (minimum $150–$200)	$
e.	Spending money, $ a week times 30 weeks equals $	$
f.	Caution money for emergencies (at least $200)	$
g.	Transportation costs	$
h.	Clothes	$
i.	Other items, such as possible medical and dental expenses, Christmas presents, etc.	$

TOTAL $_____

Q. What are colleges expecting from today's high school graduates?

A. According to a report by the College Board, sponsor of the major college entrance examination in the U.S., high school graduates should be able to write a "standard English sentence" and "use effectively the mathematics of algebra and geometry." They should also be able to use a foreign language and understand the role of computers in modern times. The report also emphasized the importance of the arts, claiming that this dimension of education can "challenge and extend the human experience."

Q. If going to college is presently out of the question, how can I further my education?

A. Correspondence courses are available. Many of these courses can be taken for college credit. For information write:

National University Continuing Education Association
One Dupont Circle, Suite 420
Washington, D.C. 20036

More information can be obtained by ordering the "Directory of Accredited Private Home Study Schools" from:

National Home Study Council
1601 18th Street
Washington, D.C. 20009

Q. I've had my fill of school and formal education. I'd like to do something with my hands. Where can I get information on job opportunities that offer training programs and apprenticeships?

A. Contact the local branch office of your State Employment Security Commission to set up an appointment for aptitude testing and/or vocational counseling. That office will also have a listing of various job opportunities and apprenticeship programs available in your area of interest.

Employers in your city probably have an association that keeps an up-to-date listing of openings, along with job descriptions and on-the-job training opportunities.

Some corporations offer excellent trainee programs, including aptitude testing and apprenticeships in a wide variety of jobs.

Q. What are the alternatives for high school graduates who are seeking to live meaningful, productive lives, but who do not plan to go to college?

A. 1. Practical training is necessary to start a career. This "vocational" training is offered by trade schools and community colleges. Check your public library for resources on (1) kinds of jobs available, (2) where various kinds of work are performed, (3) what qualifications and training are needed, (4) salaries and working conditions, (5) obtainability of various jobs in the future, and (6) where further information is available.

2. Apprenticeship in a trade may be the route to a satisfying job. As an apprentice you would have a full-time job while you learn the skills of your trade.

3. Military service, with its advantages and disadvantages, is another alternative.

4. Other options include volunteer service, a year of traveling (if you have the finances!), and working to save money for some more specialized training in the future.

You are fortunate to live in a nation that provides its young people with many ways to find personal fulfillment. With God's guidance you can find training and work that are suited to your abilities and interests. And there has never been a time in the history of our country when Christian youth were more needed in every area of its professional-vocational life.

10

Go Claim Your Mountain

A great scene is described in the fourteenth chapter of Joshua. Having crossed over the River Jordan into Canaan, the Israelites now await their inheritance. Joshua, their great leader, stands before them and gives to each tribe its inheritance, according to the Lord's command to Moses.

Then an individual breaks rank and strides confidently toward Joshua. The two men meet and stand in full sight of the great multitude. Everyone recognizes the other man as Caleb, whose heroics were known to every family.

Caleb had come with a claim to make. He had been living with a dream for a long time. Now that dream was about to come true. He reminds Joshua of the time when they both were much younger. They and ten other men had been chosen as representatives of each of the tribes to spy out the land of Canaan. Upon their return only Joshua and Caleb believed it was possible for their people to possess the land that "flowed with milk and honey," the land that God had promised the Jewish nation.

Because of the way they exercised their faith, the two men were greatly blessed by God. Joshua became

Moses' successor and Caleb, a trusted and courageous soldier and leader.

But somehow, Caleb kept remembering a beautiful place he had seen while spying out the land. The place was called Hebron. "One day," he often thought to himself, "I'll have Hebron for my own."

The day had come. At last the great moment was here and Caleb speaks: " . . . I am still as strong today as in the day Moses sent me out; I am just as vigorous to go out to battle now as I was then. Now give me this hill country . . . " (Josh. 14:11, 12a). What confidence! What a claim!

Caleb's belief in his ability to accomplish things needs to be shared by every high school graduate. The following anonymous poem tells why.

> If you think you are beaten, you are,
>   If you think you dare not, you don't,
> If you'd like to win, but you think you can't,
>   It's almost a cinch you won't.
>
> If you think you'll lose, you're lost,
>   For out in the world we find
> Success begins with a fellow's will,
>   It's all in the state of mind.
>
> If you think you're outclassed, you are,
>   you 've got to think high to rise,
> You've got to be sure of yourself before
>   You can ever win a prize.
>
> Life's battle doesn't always go
>   To the swifter or faster man,
> But sooner or later the man who wins
>   Is the man "who thinks he can."

"Everything is possible for him who believes," said Jesus (Mark 9:23). Is this just good reading, or does it really work? Those who have tried it have

> conquered kingdoms
> > administered justice
> > > gained what was promised
> > > > shut the mouths of lions
> > > > > quenched the fury of the flames
> > > > > > escaped the edge of the sword
> > > > > > > whose weakness was turned to
> > > > > > > strength
> > > > > > > > became powerful in battle
> > > > > > > > > —Hebrews 11:33, 34

This kind of attitude was demonstrated by an eighteen-year-old who wrote the following letter to Ann Landers:

> Dear Ann Landers:
> I am an 18-year-old who has something to say to "Feisty Michigander" and anyone else who thinks today's teen-agers are cream puffs with no stress in our lives and no ambition. As you would say, "Wake up and smell the coffee!"
> I live in a well-to-do suburb of Denver. Within the last four years I have seen ten classmates die from drug overdoses or suicide. Five classmates became pregnant. Dozens of my friends became addicted to cocaine. At least double that number are beer drunks. Several have told me that their parents get bombed or stoned every night. A few weeks ago, a junior high kid went on a shooting rampage and killed three people. Divorce and unemployment are so common that I am considered lucky by my peers because my parents are still

married and working. If you don't consider this
stressful, please tell me what is.

As for the part about teen-agers not working
hard, I am living proof that many of us take our
studies seriously. I will graduate in 1990 with a 4.0
grade point average.—K.B., Littleton, Colo.

Dear Little:
I know that there are many highly motivated,
straight, serious-minded teen-agers around because
I have met them, and thousands have written to
me. I am optimistic about the future, and it will be
students such as you who will make the difference.

This quality of confidence has to be learned. Those
who have a mountain they want to claim must
struggle with doubt, failure, and discouragement.

In a certain classroom at Exeter, New Hampshire, a
youth was asked to give an oral report to his
classmates. Each attempt ended in a humiliating
failure. Recalling his experience he confessed: "I could
not speak before the school. Many a piece did I
commit to memory, and recite and rehearse in my
own room, over and over again, and yet, when the
day came, when my name was called, and all eyes
turned to my seat, I could not raise myself from it.
When the occasion was over, I went home and wept
bitter tears of mortification." Later the youth decided
that he would conquer his timidity if it killed him.
Did he succeed? To know his name is to have the
answer—Daniel Webster, still acclaimed by many as
the greatest orator in American history.

Caleb's extraordinary confidence led to an extraordinary conquest. Doesn't it always? It so happened
that Hebron was the most heavily fortified area in all

of Canaan. Three great giants and their people had been successful in defeating all would-be conquerors until Caleb came along!

Caleb was given divine help because he "followed the Lord wholeheartedly." So will you! Of all the tribes given inheritances, only Caleb's completely conquered the enemy. He was not going to live with "what might have been." His claim was great; his confidence unfailing; his conquest complete. Joshua 14:13–14 gives the thrilling result of Caleb's inspiring faith: "Then Joshua blessed Caleb . . . and gave him Hebron as his inheritance . . . because he followed the Lord . . . wholeheartedly."

How about *your* "Hebron"? You, too, can claim your mountain! These can be yours: a radiant Christian influence, highly developed talents, high ideals, a well-furnished mind, singleness of purpose, a Christlike personality, unfailing tact, deep understanding and compassion, and above all, eternal life.

In these days of quick fixes, cultism, and fast living through fast spending, the passion is for pleasure, the quest is for convenience, and the search is for security. But the mountains challenge only the courageous.

Listen to the poet:

> Bring me men to match my mountains,
>   Bring me men to match my plains;
> Men with empires in their purpose,
>   And new eras in their brains.
> —Sam Walter Foss

There is a divine purpose for your life. Out there somewhere is your Hebron. As you look at it think about these stirring words from the great Phillips

Brooks: "Oh, do not pray for easy lives. Pray to be strong men and women. Do not pray for tasks equal to your powers. Pray for powers equal to your tasks. Then the doing of your work will be no miracle; but you shall be a miracle. Every day you shall wonder at yourself, at the richness of life which has come to you by the grace of God."

Consider your resources. You have infinite power behind you, Christ's abiding presence within you, and divine purpose guiding you. Your tassel has been moved and you are on your way. Consider this counsel from Martin Luther, the great reformer, who exclaimed, "Oh! how great and glorious a thing it is to have before one the Word of God! With that we may at all times feel joyous and secure; we need never be in want of consolation, for we see before us, in all its brightness, the pure and right way."

Everything you need for successful mountain-claiming has been provided. You have moved the tassel and your "Hebron" awaits your claim. Remember as you begin your journey that "in all things God works for the good of those who love him, who have been called according to his purpose. . . . What, then, shall we say in response to this? If God is for us, who can be against us? He who did not spare his own Son, but gave him up for us all—how will he not also, along with him, graciously give us all things?" (Rom. 8:28, 31, 32).

After you move the tassel, you are ready to begin the next stage of your life. The ceremony recognizing your achievement by awarding you a diploma is rightly called a *commencement;* it is a "beginning." Your high school days are over and now the un-traveled road stretches out before you.

School years are like the rungs of a ladder, and graduation looks like the top rung. But when you reach it, guess what? You realize something important about the process of growth. The rung of a ladder is not designed for long rests or stopping. It should only serve to hold your foot long enough to help you to climb one rung higher. Isn't this what growth is—moving up life's ladder, purposefully pausing at each rung long enough to step up to the next one? No rung on this ladder was meant to rest upon very long—not even graduation. If you are going to become what you're capable of becoming and achieve what you're capable of achieving, keep moving up!

If you are going to continue to experience this process of growth, you are going to have to reject some of the advice that's probably written in your high school annual. Looking at mine, and many others, I read such well-meaning but terribly wrong advice, such as, "Always stay just as you are." Actually, only by going beyond where you are will you grow into the kind of person you are capable of becoming. For becoming all that God gifted you to become, you will find no better guideline than the Scripture text quoted at the beginning of this book:

> Trust in the Lord with all your heart
> > and lean not on your own understanding;
> in all your ways acknowledge him,
> > and he will make your paths straight.
> > > —Proverbs 3:5, 6

11

Yes, No, and Whoopee!

Graduating seniors are moving in the right direction if they're able to say "Yes, No, and Whoopee!"

Let's take a closer look at that and change its order to start with the no. Today's tassel-movers are getting great amounts of advice emphasizing this powerful little word—no. Say no to drugs. Say no to quick fixes, shortcuts, and easy choices. It's a vitally important word. If it's spoken at the right time in the right situation in the right way to the right person(s), it can give your heart a song that will last for the rest of your life. Failure to say no can strike a tragically different tune—addiction, loss of control, unwanted pregnancy, poor preparation, missed opportunity, and low self-esteem. There's very little joyous melody in a song we are forced to sing because we chose not to say no.

Failure to say no can lead to experiencing the following:

So little man you've grown tired of grass,
    LSD, goofballs, cocaine and hash.
And someone said, pretending to be a true friend,
    "I'll introduce you to Miss Heroin."
Well honey, before you start fooling around with
    me,
    Just let me inform you of how it will be.
For I will seduce you and make you my slave,
    I've sent men much stronger than you to their
    grave.
You think you could never become a disgrace,
    And end up addicted to poppy seed waste.
So you'll start inhaling me one afternoon,
    You'll take me into your arms very soon.
And once I have entered deep down in your vein,
    The craving will drive you deeply insane.
You'll need lots of money (for you have been told),
    I'm much more expensive than purest gold.
You'll turn into something vile and corrupt,
    You'll swindle your mother and just for a buck.
You'll mug and steal for my narcotic charm,
    And feel contentment when I'm in your arm.
The day when you realize the monster you've
    grown,
    You'll solemnly promise to leave me alone.
If you think that you've got the mystical knack,
    Then sweetie just get me off your back.
The vomit, the cramps, your gut tied in a knot,
    The jangling nerves screaming for just one more
    shot.
The hot chills and cold sweat, the withdrawal pains,
    Can only be saved by my little white grains.
There's no other way and no need to look,
    For deep down inside, you know you're hooked.
You'll desperately run to the pusher and then,
    You'll welcome me back to your arms again.

And when you return just as I foretold,
    I know that you'll give me your body and soul.
You'll give up your morals, your conscience, your
        heart,
    And you will be mine until death do us part.

And it all starts with a failure to say no!

A prominent pastor shared his experience with a young man who came to him for counseling. The youth told his pastor that some friends had been a bad influence on his life. They enjoyed going to a particular club where they could get plenty of drugs, and he would go with them even though he had often promised himself and God that he would stop. He explained to his pastor that in spite of all his best intentions, he could not stop going with his friends and taking drugs. Now he was in the pastor's study hoping that the pastor had an answer for him. And the pastor *did* indeed have an answer for him, but it was not the quick fix that the youth had expected. For the pastor simply said, "Son, why don't you stop?"

"I can't," he replied.

"What do you mean you can't stop?" asked the pastor. "You're the one who goes there. Nobody forces you. You're the one who takes the drugs. Nobody puts a gun to your head and makes you take them. So just stop."

"You know," replied the surprised youth, "nobody ever put it to me that way." Three weeks later the young man called his pastor and said, "You gave me the best advice I have ever received. You said stop and I did. I haven't touched drugs since I talked with you."

Choices! We *can* choose! We *can* change! We *can* choose to stop doing what is wrong, bad, foolish, and inappropriate. We *can* choose to start what is right, good, smart, and mature! Easy? No. Possible? Yes.

Freedom to choose means that I *can* let peer pressure control me. I *can* experiment with drugs and alcohol. I *can* compromise my moral standards. I *can* choose the quick, easy way. God gives us the freedom to choose. But when we exercise this freedom to choose, we must realize we are *not* free to control the consequence of our choices. Because we reap what we sow, we must understand where the problem starts and where it can lead. The following has it in a nutshell:

> Sow a thought, reap an act
> Sow an act, reap a habit
> Sow a habit, reap a character
> Sow a character, reap a destiny

Serious drug addiction requires professional help. Christ-centered hospitalization programs are available. But before it gets that far, you do have a choice.

A new lineman with a professional football team was playing his first game. Coming off the field he complained to his coach that he was having a problem with the opposing lineman. "Coach, he keeps pulling my helmet over my eyes. What should I do?"

"Don't let him do it," replied the coach.

We are not victims unless we choose to think of ourselves that way.

When John Wesley questioned his mother along these lines she gave him this advice: "Would you judge of the lawfulness or unlawfulness of pleasure? Take this rule: Whatever weakens your reason, impairs the tenderness of your conscience, obscures your sense of God, or takes off the relish of spiritual things; in short, whatever increases the strength and authority of your body over your mind, that thing is sin to you, however innocent it may be in itself."

Saying no is important, but not enough. Stopping what we ought to stop is necessary but falls short of an adequate answer. A simple story Jesus told long ago explains why. A man had an evil spirit that left him. Later it returned and found the "house" empty. So it went out and found seven other spirits more wicked than itself and they all returned to the empty house and moved in. Tragically, the man's life became worse than before (cf. Matt. 12:43–45).

The lesson is clear. Sweeping the house clean by getting rid of what is bad is not enough. If we major in the negatives—what we *can't* do, where we *can't* go—our life's curriculum fails us. That is why Jesus told the story of the empty house. He wanted us to know that the power for living is in what we say yes to. Saying a big enough yes to what is right, good, and true is the best way to say no to what is wrong, bad, and false.

From Greek mythology comes the story of Ulysses and the Sirens (beautiful sea nymphs) who sang so bewitchingly that sailors could not resist sailing to their island. Many ships were destroyed and many men died as the Sirens lured them to their destruction. All kinds of strategies were tried to resist the Sirens' tempting songs. Some sailors had themselves tied to the ship's mast, but that didn't work. Others tried stuffing their ears with wax, and that failed too.

Finally, Ulysses discovered a better way. He invited Orpheus on board their ship. When they approached the Sirens' island, he began to sing, and his song was more beautiful than the songs of the Sirens. That is the strategy that wins. When Christ is on board our ship, we have the loveliest music known to the human heart. "The one who is in you is greater than the one who is in the world" (1 John 4:4).

Say yes to the development of love, joy, peace, patience, kindness, goodness, faithfulness, gentleness, and self-control. These characteristics are admired by all sensible people, even those who don't believe in God. Take self-control, for example. It would be hard to imagine a commencement exercise anywhere in this nation in which the speakers failed to stress the importance of developing greater control over ourselves. Lack of self-control underlies the misuse of our freedom to choose. Religious leaders, educators, politicians, mental health authorities, law enforcement officials, and parents are all asking the same question: What's the answer to the problem of *control?*

Thoughtful tassel-movers realize that to get the answer to this vitally important question we must be able to accurately connect the effects—lack of control, hostility, injustice, violence, meaninglessness, and hopelessness—with their cause.

We are making a good start by understanding that we are part of a "cut-flower generation." The virtues of love, joy, peace, patience, kindness, goodness, faithfulness, gentleness, and self-control are like flowers cut from their roots. These virtues are still found in our society but are severed from their living source—Christ. Like flowers no longer connected to life-giving roots and soil, these virtues sooner or later will wither and die. Our society's dilemma is the result of not knowing that all these virtues so highly valued by enlightened minds are spiritually connected to Christ, who said, "I am the way, the truth and the life" (John 14:6). To try to preserve what has been separated from the living source leads to the confusion and despair of our times.

Say yes to service. Recently President Bush spoke to some three thousand children and teenagers who had been invited to the South Lawn at the White House. His message went straight from the shoulder: "Make it your mission to make a difference in somebody else's life."

He stated, "A single fact in America today is that too many people are free-falling through society, with no prospect of landing on their feet. No one—young, old, white, brown, or black—should be permitted to go through life unclaimed."

Helping others, Bush explained, gives meaning and adventure to life and is something to start "when you're young and stick with it all life long." Bush stressed that everyone has something to offer. "Kids from tough neighborhoods have grown up on food stamps and hand-me-downs. And maybe you think you've got nothing anyone wants. You're wrong.

"I've asked you here today . . . because I need your help, because America needs your help," the president told his youthful audience. To show the seriousness of our national concerns, Bush cited the statistics of what's happening to America's youth, to "kids like you." He said that on a typical day:

Almost 1,700 high school students drop out.

Over 4,000 teenagers run away from home.[*]
More than 2,700 teens become pregnant.
Over a dozen will commit suicide.

Bush told the students of an earlier time in the nation's history when the church steeple bells rang in time of need and how people came to help without asking who needed it or why. "The bells have been silent too long," he said. "I call on you to commit yourselves, listen to the bells, make it your mission to make a difference in somebody else's life."

The president invited them to join his Youth Engaged in Service to America, or YES. He stressed that his YES program is voluntary. "You don't need to be bribed with incentives and threatened with penalties to get engaged in community service. . . . Service is its own reward."

You can be part of a greatly needed movement of young people who understand that the answer to our war on drugs, alcoholism, violence, sexual permissiveness, and crime lies in experiencing personally the living relationship with Christ. Being biblically related to Christ is the only way to have the insight and strength to say "Yes, No, and Whoopee!"

In Marc Connelly's play, *The Green Pastures*, the archangel Gabriel becomes impatient with humankind and pleads with God to let him sound the trumpet and bring in Judgment Day. With a gentle rebuke God reminds him: "Gabriel, have you noticed

---

[*]More than 5,000 teenagers a year are buried in unmarked graves and more than a million teenage runaways are on the streets of our major cities (*Newsweek*, April 25, 1988).

that every now and then mankind turns out some pretty good specimens?"

Turning out "pretty good specimens!" It happens when we can say a big enough yes to a God who believes in us, who cares for us, and who offers us a way of life worthy of our best. What other response could be given to the invitation in 1 Peter 5:7: "Casting the whole of your care—all your anxieties, all your concerns, once and for all—on Him, for He cares for you affectionately, and cares about you watchfully" (Amplified Version).

A prominent English minister recalled the turning point in his life when he was seventeen years old. "I was called the black sheep of the family," he said. And one night he and his family got into one of their frequent fights. He felt that they were all against him—his father, mother, brother, and sister. He took it as long as he could and finally jumped up and cried, "I'm leaving; I'm getting out of here." He ran up the stairs, and there in the darkened hallway he ran into his grandmother. She had heard the whole bitter exchange. As he approached her, she put her hand on his shoulder. With tears in her eyes she said these words that changed his life: "John, I believe in you."

Saying no and yes brings us to whoopee—the last part of our definition of the person growing in the right direction. Those who can say whoopee know how to *celebrate* life. Without ignoring life's trials, temptations, and difficult challenges, these fortunate individuals find special meaning in the common, ordinary things of life. Although they plan for the future and discipline themselves in the present, they enjoy the life they have now. Others enjoy being around them because this attitude is positively contagious.

Celebrating life is possible when life is meaningful, purposeful, and productive. The celebrative attitude allows for disappointment, failure, confusion, and mistreatment, and it rises above difficult, painful circumstances. When it rains on your parade, a celebrative approach keeps you optimistic without forcing you to deny that the rain is falling. You can focus on your strengths and be aware of your weaknesses. You can keep your perspective without losing sight of your problems. You can set realistic goals while experiencing a failure! You can learn to live *toward* the unfamiliar even as you feel afraid, insecure, or undeserving of success. You can seek help when you need it, knowing that sometimes life gets too big for any of us to handle alone. Sooner or later, the smartest, strongest, and bravest need others.

Your ability to celebrate life as you are called upon to live it stretches with the knowledge that God knows you, loves you, believes in you, and has allowed you to have your life. So live it to the fullest, saying yes to what is right, no to what is wrong, and whoopee! because you not only have life, but as a Christian, you have a personal relationship with him who gave it!

This growing ability to say "Yes, No, and Whoopee" depends on our being able to experience the truth of one of Christ's most unforgettable statements, "I have come that they may have life, and have it to the full" (John 10:10).